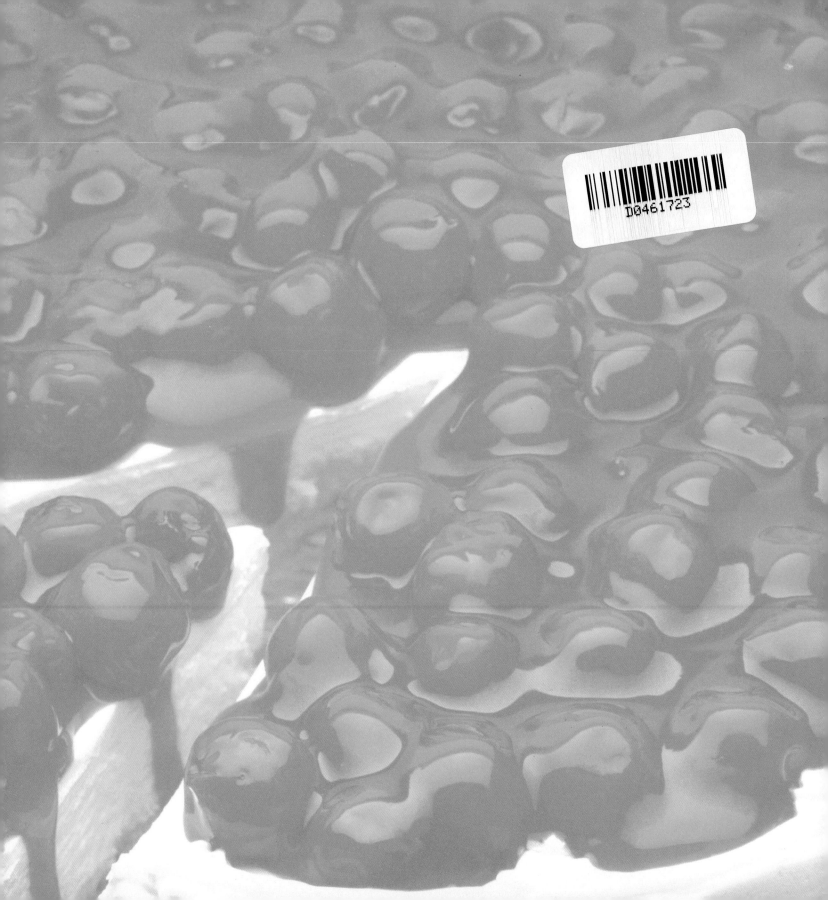

home *cooking*

p

This is a Parragon Publishing Book
First published in 2004

Parragon Publishing
Queen Street House
4 Queen Street
Bath
BA1 1HE
United Kingdom

Created and produced by *The Bridgewater Book Company Ltd*.

ISBN: 1-40543-798-7

Printed in China

NOTES FOR THE READER

This book uses imperial, metric, and US cup measurements. Follow the same units of measurement throughout; do not mix imperial and metric. All spoon measurements are level: teaspoons are assumed to be 5 ml, and tablespoons are assumed to be 15 ml. Unless otherwise stated, milk is assumed to be whole, eggs and individual vegetables such as potatoes are medium, and pepper is freshly ground black pepper.

Recipes using raw or very lightly cooked eggs should be avoided by infants, the elderly, pregnant women, convalescents, and anyone suffering from an illness. Pregnant and breastfeeding women are advised to avoid eating peanuts and peanut products. The times given are an approximate guide only, and may vary according to the techniques and equipment used by different people.

contents

introduction

Despite our busy lives today everybody still loves good home cooked food and it rightly occupies a central place in our hearts and on our tables. However, too often we settle for a delivery pizza because summoning up the energy to cook "real" food seems like too much effort. With this book, the problem is solved. It features recipes that are easy to prepare, use widely available ingredients, and are often made in minutes. Homemade meals are also tasty, filling, and can be wonderfully restorative to the body and soul.

A home cooked meal is something to look forward to and savor. It is possible to fit wholesome, easy meals using fresh and inexpensive ingredients into a busy or stressful lifestyle. It is also the perfect antidote for days when everything has gone wrong! Maybe the bus was late, it was raining, and you forgot your umbrella; a quick midweek home cooked meal is then a relaxing and comforting end to the day. Home cooked food is also perfect for when you want to unwind at the weekend with a lazy brunch or a

long, relaxing supper featuring familiar and favourite dishes. Home cooking is loved by people of all ages and so is ideal and enjoyable for families, or just as a treat for yourself while relaxing on a Sunday morning.

This book is divided into five chapters to make choosing your home cooked dishes as easy as possible. The first offers easy-to-make midweek dishes. Many just need assembling and popping in the oven, where they will cook to perfection while you put your feet up. The second chapter provides ideas for those times when you need something heartwarming, either because the weather is cheerless or because you're feeling bleak. Filling soups, substantial stews, and steamed puddings fit the bill.

Unwind at the weekend by taking your time to enjoy the recipes in the third chapter. Follow a long lie-in with a scrumptious brunch of homemade soup, or relax after the household chores with a long and lazy supper. The chapter of family favorites features all those well-loved goodies that we crave but never admit to liking in public. We all deserve an extra-special treat sometimes and the final chapter offers the ultimate in homemade desserts featuring chocolate. Its cakes, mousses, trifles, and homemade fudge will take you out of this world.

The enjoyment of home cooked food can only be increased by the knowledge that it is the healthiest, most economical way to eat—as well as fun and easy to cook.

home cooking

Some people are put off home cooking by the amount of preparation they think they need to do to produce a homemade meal. A few helpful hints can take the pain out of preparation and make it as enjoyable as the final result!

Keep your pantry stocked up with a good supply of all the staples. Canned goods, from tomatoes to tuna, are perfect for all kinds of satisfying dishes. Canned beans also help provide the basis for a flavorful meal and don't require lengthy soaking before cooking. Packages of rice, pasta, and noodles provide almost-instant carbohydrate, which is in itself comfort food because it fills you up and gives you slow-release energy. Sugar, flour, cornstarch, unsweetened cocoa, and dried fruit all form an excellent basis for numerous tasty treats for the sweet-toothed.

Make the most of your freezer. Not only is it worth keeping a supply of basic ingredients, such as frozen vegetables, fish, and meat, you can also stock up on comfort foods that you have cooked in advance. Stews and casseroles, in particular, often taste even better after keeping than they do on the day you make them. When you're feeling energetic, cook a batch of Speedy Chili Beef (see page 66) or Chicken, Sausage & Bean Stew (see page 42) and freeze them in individual portions for those times when you want a quick fix of

a substantial meal knowing that you have already done the preparation. Buying some special goodies for the freezer, such as jumbo shrimp, when you're feeling extravagant (or it's pay day) ensures that you have the ingredients for a special treat when comfort food is the

order of the day. Don't forget that frozen pie dough is a great standby for both sweet and savory tarts and pies. Do remember to keep an eye on "use-by" dates.

Keep kitchen equipment in good order to minimize the effort involved in preparing home cooked food. Keep knives sharp to speed up slicing and chopping and reduce the risk of accidents. Good quality, heavy-bottom pans can safely be left with their contents simmering while you slip into something comfortable without the worry that supper will burn. An ovenproof casserole is very easy for one-pot dishes and reduces dish washing—definitely an advantage. A reliable can opener—and, possibly, corkscrew—is a must.

Although it's always sensible to plan in advance, the recipes in this book use all kinds of meat, poultry, fish, and vegetables, so you can simply buy your favorites when shopping for fresh goods. They're also very adaptable, meaning it's easy to substitute ingredients

that you prefer or just happen to have at hand this particular week. If you haven't got turkey for the pie, use chicken or even pork; if you haven't got a fresh chili, crush a dried one or use flakes.

The joy of home cooking is not simply in the eating, but in its versatility and the ease with which you can prepare and cook it.

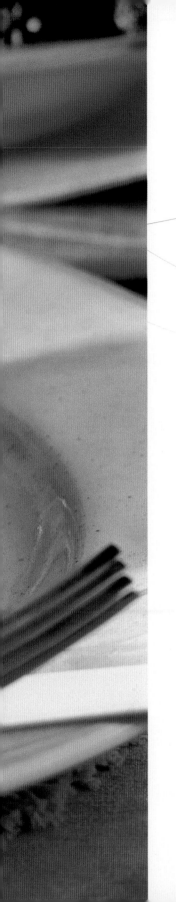

CHAPTER I

week days:

chill out /
TV dinners

baked fish & french fries

INGREDIENTS

1 lb/450 g mealy potatoes, cut into thick,
even-size french fries
vegetable oil spray
scant ¹/₂ cup all-purpose flour
1 egg
1 cup fresh white bread crumbs, seasoned to
taste with salt and pepper
4 cod or haddock fillets

TO GARNISH
lemon wedges
fresh parsley sprigs

SERVES 4

Preheat the oven to 400°F/200°C. Line 2 baking sheets with nonstick liner.

Rinse the potatoes under cold running water, then dry well on a clean dish towel. Put in a bowl, spray with oil, and toss together until coated. Spread the french fries on a baking sheet and cook in the oven for 40–45 minutes, turning once, until golden.

Meanwhile, put the flour on a plate, beat the egg in a shallow dish, and spread the seasoned bread crumbs on a large plate. Dip the fish fillets in the flour to coat, then the egg (allowing any excess to drip off) and finally the bread crumbs, patting them firmly into the fish. Place the fish in one layer on a baking sheet.

Fifteen minutes before the french fries have cooked bake the fish fillets in the oven for 10–15 minutes, turning them once during cooking, until the fish is tender. Serve the fish with the french fries, garnished with lemon wedges and parsley sprigs.

INGREDIENTS

4 large baking potatoes
3 oz/85 g butter
1 large garlic clove, crushed
5 1/2 oz/150 g mushrooms, sliced
1 tbsp snipped fresh chives
2 tbsp chopped fresh parsley
salt and pepper
3/4 cup heavy cream

4 tbsp grated Cheddar cheese
4 tbsp chopped lightly toasted
    walnuts, to garnish
fresh mixed salad, to serve

baked *potatoes* with cream *&* walnuts

SERVES 4

Preheat the oven to 375°F/190°C. Scrub the potatoes and pierce the skins several times with a fork. Place on a baking sheet and bake in the oven for 1 1/4 hours, or until cooked through. About 5 minutes before the end of the cooking time, melt 1 1/2 tablespoons of the butter in a skillet over low heat, add the garlic and mushrooms, and cook, stirring, for 4 minutes, or until the mushrooms are tender. Remove from the heat and set aside.

Remove the potatoes from the oven and cut them in half lengthwise. Carefully scoop out the potato flesh into a bowl, leaving the skins intact. Add the remaining butter to the potato flesh, then stir in the herbs. Season to taste with salt and pepper. Spoon the mixture into the potato skins, then add a layer of mushrooms. Top with the cream, then the cheese. Return the potatoes to the oven and bake for an additional 10 minutes at the same temperature. Remove from the oven, sprinkle over the walnuts, and serve with a mixed salad.

INGREDIENTS

scant 8$^{1}/_{2}$ cups stock or water
1 tbsp olive oil
3 tbsp butter
1 small onion, finely chopped
1 lb/450 g risotto rice
salt and pepper
$^{1}/_{2}$ cup freshly grated
   Parmesan cheese or Grana Padano,
   plus shavings to garnish

basic *risotto*

SERVES 4

Bring the stock to a boil, then reduce the heat and keep simmering
gently over low heat while you are cooking the risotto. Heat the oil with
2 tablespoons of the butter in a deep pan over medium heat until the butter
has melted. Stir in the onion and cook gently until soft and starting to turn
golden. Do not brown.

Add the rice and mix to coat in the oil and butter. Cook and stir for
2–3 minutes, or until the grains are translucent. Gradually add the stock,
a ladle at a time. Stir constantly and add more liquid as the rice absorbs
it. Increase the heat to medium so that the liquid bubbles. Cook for
20 minutes, or until all the liquid is absorbed. Season to taste with salt and
pepper but don't add too much salt as the Parmesan cheese is salty. The
risotto should be of a creamy consistency with a bit of bite in the rice.

Remove the risotto from the heat and add the remaining butter. Mix well,
then stir in the Parmesan cheese until it melts. Taste and adjust the
seasoning, then serve, garnished with Parmesan cheese shavings.

pizza *dough* & pizza *topping*

INGREDIENTS

scant 1⁵/₈ cups white bread flour,
plus extra for dusting
1 tsp active dry yeast
1 tsp salt
2 tbsp olive oil
1–1¹/₂ cups warm water

TOPPING
4 tbsp olive oil
1 large onion, thinly sliced
6 white mushrooms,
thinly sliced
¹/₂ small green bell pepper, ¹/₂ small red bell
pepper, and ¹/₂ small yellow bell pepper,
seeded and thinly sliced
10¹/₂ oz/300 g ready-made
tomato pasta sauce
2 oz/55 g mozzarella cheese,
thickly sliced
2 tbsp freshly grated Parmesan cheese
1 tsp chopped fresh basil

fresh crisp salad, to serve

SERVES 2

Combine the flour, yeast, and salt in a mixing bowl. Drizzle over half the oil. Make a well in the center and pour in the water. Mix to a firm dough and shape into a ball. Turn out onto a floured counter and knead until it is no longer sticky. Oil the bowl with the remaining oil. Put the dough into the bowl and turn to coat with oil. Cover with a dish towel and let rise for 1 hour.

When the dough has doubled in size, punch it down to release the excess air, then knead until smooth. Divide in half and roll into 2 thin circles. Place on a baking sheet.

Preheat the oven to 425°F/220°C. For the topping, soften the vegetables for 5 minutes in the oil. Spread some of the tomato sauce over the pizza bases, but do not go right to the edge. Top with the vegetables and mozzarella cheese. Spoon over more tomato sauce, then sprinkle with Parmesan cheese and chopped basil. Bake for 10 minutes, or until the base is crispy and the cheese has melted. Serve with a crisp salad.

INGREDIENTS

6 eggs
4 tbsp milk
salt and pepper
1 lb/450 g potatoes
2 tbsp olive oil
2 tbsp butter
2 onions, finely chopped
1 green or red bell pepper, seeded
  and finely chopped
fresh parsley sprigs, to garnish

spanish *omelet*

SERVES 4

In a bowl, beat the eggs, milk, and salt and pepper to taste together. Cut the potatoes into $^{1}/_{2}$-inch/1-cm cubes.

Heat the oil and butter in a large skillet. Add the potatoes, onions, and bell pepper and cook very slowly for 10–15 minutes, stirring occasionally, until almost cooked. Increase the heat and cook for an additional 5–10 minutes, or until the vegetables start to brown.

Preheat the broiler to high. Pour in the egg mixture and cook over low heat for 5 minutes, or until the mixture is set and the underside is golden brown.

Transfer the skillet to the broiler and cook until the top is set and golden brown. Garnish the omelet with parsley sprigs and serve it hot, cut into wedges.

INGREDIENTS

1 red onion, sliced into thick rings
1 small eggplant, thickly sliced
2 large mushrooms, halved
3 red bell peppers, halved and seeded
3 plum tomatoes, peeled and diced
salt and pepper
2 garlic cloves, minced
1 tbsp chopped fresh
  flat-leaf parsley
1 tsp chopped fresh rosemary

1 tsp dried thyme or oregano
finely grated rind of 1 lemon
scant $1/4$ cup stale, coarse bread
  crumbs
3 tbsp olive oil, plus extra
  for brushing
6–8 black olives, pitted and sliced
1 oz/25 g feta cheese
  (drained weight), cut into
  $1/2$-inch/1-cm cubes

baked mediterranean *vegetables* with feta

SERVES 4

Preheat the broiler to medium. Put the onion, eggplant, mushrooms, and
bell peppers on a large baking sheet, placing the bell peppers cut-side
down. Brush lightly with oil.

Cook under the broiler for 10–12 minutes, turning the onion, eggplant, and
mushrooms halfway through, until starting to blacken. Cut into even-size
chunks. Place in a shallow ovenproof dish. Arrange the diced tomatoes on
top and season to taste with salt and pepper.

Preheat the oven to 425°F/220°C.

In a bowl, combine the garlic, parsley, rosemary, thyme, and lemon rind
with the bread crumbs. Season to taste with pepper. Add the oil to bind the
mixture together. Sprinkle the mixture over the vegetables and add the
olives and cheese.

Bake in the oven for 10–15 minutes, or until the vegetables are heated
through and the topping is crisp. Serve straight from the dish.

mushroom &cauliflower cheese *crumble*

INGREDIENTS

salt and pepper
1 medium cauliflower
2 oz/55 g butter, plus 2 tbsp
for the topping
4 oz/115 g white mushrooms, sliced
1 cup dry bread crumbs
2 tbsp freshly grated Parmesan cheese
1 tsp dried oregano
1 tsp dried parsley

SERVES 4

Preheat the oven to 450°F/230°C.

Break the cauliflower into small florets. Bring a large pan of salted water to a boil and cook the florets in the boiling water for 3 minutes. Remove from the heat, drain well, and transfer to a large shallow ovenproof dish.

Melt the 2 oz/55 g butter in a small skillet over medium heat. Add the mushrooms, stir to coat, and cook gently for 3 minutes. Remove from the heat and add to the cauliflower. Season to taste with salt and pepper.

Combine the bread crumbs, cheese, and herbs in a small mixing bowl, then sprinkle the crumbs over the vegetables.

Dice the butter for the topping and dot over the crumbs.

Place the dish in the oven and bake for 15 minutes, or until the crumbs are golden brown and crisp. Serve straight from the dish.

INGREDIENTS

3 tbsp butter

1 small onion, finely chopped

6 scallions, green part included,
   finely chopped

4 potatoes, cut into chunks

3 cups chicken stock

salt and pepper

2/3 cup milk

2/3 cup whipping cream

2 tbsp chopped fresh
   flat-leaf parsley

scant 3/4 cup coarsely grated
   Cheddar cheese

fresh flat-leaf parsley leaves,
   to garnish

fried garlic croutons, to serve
   (optional)

creamy potato, onion & cheese *soup*

SERVES 4

Heat the butter in a large pan over medium heat. Add the onion, scallions, and potatoes. Cover and cook for 5–7 minutes, or until the onions are just tender.

Add the stock. Bring to a boil, then cover and let simmer over medium–low heat for 15–20 minutes, or until the potatoes are tender. Remove from the heat.

Mash the potatoes and season to taste with salt and pepper. Stir in the milk, cream, and chopped parsley. Reheat gently. Ladle into bowls and sprinkle with the cheese and parsley leaves.

Serve with garlic croutons, if desired.

INGREDIENTS

salt and pepper
1 cup dried short macaroni
1 small egg, lightly beaten
2 tbsp butter
4 small leeks, green part included,
  finely sliced
2 carrots, diced
1 tbsp all-purpose flour
1/4 tsp freshly grated nutmeg

generous 1 cup chicken stock
8 oz/225 g diced cooked turkey
  or chicken
2 oz/55 g diced ham
3 tbsp chopped fresh
  flat-leaf parsley
7/8 cup freshly grated
  Gruyère cheese

turkey, leek & cheese *gratin*

SERVES 4

Preheat the oven to 350°F/180°C.

Cook the macaroni in plenty of boiling salted water until just tender. Drain and return to the pan. Stir in the egg and a teaspoon of the butter, mixing well. Set aside.

Melt the remaining butter in a pan over medium heat. Add the leeks and carrots. Cover and cook for 5 minutes, shaking the pan occasionally, until just tender.

Add the flour and nutmeg. Cook for 1 minute, stirring constantly. Pour in the stock. Bring to a boil, stirring constantly. Stir in the turkey, ham, and parsley. Season to taste with salt and pepper.

Spread half the turkey mixture over the base of a shallow baking dish. Spread the macaroni over the turkey. Top with the remaining turkey mixture. Sprinkle with the cheese.

Bake in the oven for 15–20 minutes. Serve the gratin when the cheese is golden and bubbling.

chicken & potato *pie*

INGREDIENTS

PIE DOUGH
scant 2¹/₂ cups all-purpose flour, plus extra
for dusting
pinch of salt
6 oz/175 g butter, diced, plus extra
for greasing
about 6 tbsp cold water
milk, for brushing

FILLING
generous 1 cup chicken stock
1 lb 9 oz/700 g skinless, boneless chicken,
cut into bite-size chunks
3¹/₂ oz/100 g potatoes, coarsely chopped
1 egg, beaten
scant ⁵/₈ cup shelled hazelnuts,
toasted and ground
2³/₄ oz/75 g Cheddar cheese, grated
2 scallions, chopped
1 tbsp chopped fresh sage
salt and pepper

selection of freshly cooked vegetables,
to serve

SERVES 4

To make the pie dough, sift the flour and salt into a bowl. Rub in the butter until the mixture resembles bread crumbs. Gradually stir in enough of the cold water to make a pliable dough. Knead lightly. Cover with plastic wrap and let chill for 1 hour.

Meanwhile, to make the filling, bring the stock to a boil in a pan. Reduce the heat, add the chicken and potatoes, and let simmer for 30 minutes. Remove from the heat, let cool for 25 minutes, then drain off the liquid and transfer the chicken and potatoes to a bowl. Stir in the remaining filling ingredients.

Preheat the oven to 375°F/190°C. Grease a 9-inch/23-cm pie pan. Remove the dough from the refrigerator. On a floured counter, shape into a ball, roll out half the dough to a thickness of ¹/₄ inch/5 mm and use to line the pan. Spoon in the filling. Roll out the remaining dough to make the lid. Brush the pie rim with water, cover with the lid, and trim the edges. Cut 2 slits in the top. Add decorative shapes made from the dough trimmings. Brush with milk. Bake for 45 minutes, then serve with vegetables.

INGREDIENTS

1 lb 9 oz/700 g cod fillets

2¹/₂ cups fish stock

9 oz/250 g potatoes, sliced

salt and pepper

2 tbsp butter

1 onion, sliced

1 garlic clove, chopped

1 carrot, sliced

2 celery stalks, sliced

3¹/₂ oz/100 g cremini mushrooms, sliced

4 tomatoes, sliced

2 tbsp chopped fresh basil

1 tbsp sherry

all-purpose flour, for dusting

1 package frozen puff pastry, thawed

1 tbsp milk

TO SERVE

crisp lettuce leaves

freshly cooked snow peas

cod puff *pie*

SERVES 4

Preheat the oven to 400°F/200°C. Rinse the cod and pat dry. Bring the stock to a boil in a large pan, add the cod, and let simmer for 10 minutes. Drain, then cut into chunks. Meanwhile, cook the potatoes in salted water for 5 minutes. Drain. Melt half the butter in a skillet over low heat. Add the onion and garlic and cook for 3 minutes. Add the carrot and celery and cook for 5 minutes. Lift out the vegetables and set aside.

Melt the remaining butter in the skillet. Add the mushrooms and tomatoes and cook for 7 minutes. Stir in the basil and sherry. Cook for 1 minute. On a floured counter, roll out enough pastry to line a large pie dish, with an overhang of 1 inch/2.5 cm. Put some of the tomato mixture into the lined dish. Top with a layer of cod, then a vegetable layer, then a potato layer. Repeat the layers to fill the pie. Season to taste with salt and pepper. Top with pastry, trim, and crimp, then make a slit in the top. Decorate with fish shapes made from the dough trimmings and brush with the milk. Bake for 30 minutes. Serve with lettuce leaves and snow peas.

INGREDIENTS

2 tbsp vegetable oil

2 tbsp butter

9 oz/250 g okra, trimmed and
   thickly sliced

1 onion, finely chopped

2 celery stalks, quartered lengthwise
   and diced

1 green bell pepper, seeded and diced

2 garlic cloves, minced

7 oz/200 g canned chopped tomatoes

$^1/_2$ tsp dried thyme or oregano

1 fresh bay leaf

salt and pepper

$3^1/_2$ cups chicken stock
   or water

1 lb/450 g fresh or frozen raw
   shrimp, peeled and deveined

few drops of Tabasco sauce

2 tbsp chopped fresh cilantro,
   to garnish

shrimp *gumbo*

SERVES 4

Heat the oil and butter in a large pan over medium heat. Add the okra and
cook, uncovered, for 15 minutes, or until it loses its gummy consistency.

Add the onion, celery, bell pepper, garlic, tomatoes, thyme, and bay leaf.
Season to taste with salt and pepper. Cover and cook over medium–low
heat for 10 minutes.

Pour in the stock. Bring to a boil, then cover and let simmer over
medium–low heat for 15 minutes, or until the vegetables are al dente.
Add the shrimp and Tabasco sauce. Cook for 5 minutes, or until the
shrimp are pink.

Stir in the cilantro to garnish just before serving.

lemon meringue *pie*

PIE DOUGH
scant 1¹/₂ cups all-purpose flour, plus
extra for dusting
3¹/₂ oz/100 g butter, diced, plus extra
for greasing
scant ¹/₂ cup confectioners' sugar, sifted
finely grated rind of 1 lemon
1 egg yolk, beaten
3 tbsp milk

FILLING
3 tbsp cornstarch
1¹/₄ cups cold water
juice and grated rind of 2 lemons
⁷/₈ cup superfine sugar
2 eggs, separated

SERVES 4

To make the pie dough, sift the flour into a bowl and rub in the butter. Mix in the remaining ingredients. Knead briefly on a lightly floured counter, then let rest for 30 minutes.

Preheat the oven to 350°F/180°C. Grease an 8-inch/20-cm ovenproof pie dish. Roll out the dough to a thickness of ¹/₄ inch/5 mm and use it to line the dish. Prick with a fork, line with parchment paper, and fill with dried beans. Bake for 15 minutes. Remove from the oven. Reduce the oven temperature to 300°F/150°C.

To make the filling, mix the cornstarch with a little of the water. Put the remaining water into a pan. Stir in the lemon juice and rind and cornstarch paste. Bring to a boil, stirring. Cook for 2 minutes. Let cool slightly. Stir in 5 tablespoons of the superfine sugar and the egg yolks, then pour the mixture into the pastry shell. In a bowl, whisk the egg whites until stiff. Gradually whisk in the remaining superfine sugar and spread over the pie. Bake for 40 minutes. Remove from the oven and serve.

INGREDIENTS

PIE DOUGH
scant 1¹/2 cups all-purpose flour, plus
  extra for dusting
3¹/2 oz/100 g butter, diced, plus extra
  for greasing
scant ¹/2 cup confectioners' sugar,
  sifted
finely grated rind of 1 lemon
1 egg yolk, beaten
3 tbsp milk

FILLING
3 cooking apples
2 tbsp lemon juice
finely grated rind of 1 lemon
²/3 cup honey
3 cups fresh white or whole-wheat
  bread crumbs
1 tsp allspice
pinch of freshly grated nutmeg

whipped cream, to serve

spiced apple *tart*

SERVES 4

To make the pie dough, sift the flour into a bowl and rub in the butter. Mix
in the remaining ingredients. Knead briefly on a lightly floured counter,
then let rest for 30 minutes.

Preheat the oven to 400°F/200°C. Grease an 8-inch/20-cm tart pan. Roll out
the dough to a thickness of ¹/4 inch/5 mm and use to line the bottom and
sides of the pan.

To make the filling, core 2 of the apples and grate them into a bowl.
Add half the lemon juice and all the lemon rind, along with the honey,
bread crumbs, and allspice. Mix together well. Spoon evenly into the pastry
shell. Core and slice the remaining apple and use to decorate the top of the
tart. Brush the apple slices with the remaining lemon juice, then sprinkle
over the nutmeg. Bake in the oven for 35 minutes, or until firm. Remove
from the oven and serve with whipped cream.

INGREDIENTS

1¹/₈ cups blueberries
1¹/₈ cups raspberries
1¹/₈ cups blackberries
¹/₂ cup superfine sugar
scant 1¹/₂ cups all-purpose flour, plus
  extra for dusting
generous ¹/₄ cup ground hazelnuts
3¹/₂ oz/100 g butter, diced, plus extra
  for greasing

finely grated rind of 1 lemon
1 egg yolk, beaten
4 tbsp milk
2 tsp confectioners' sugar, for dusting
whipped cream, to serve

forest fruit *pie*

SERVES 4

Put the fruit into a pan with 3 tablespoons of the superfine sugar and
let simmer, stirring, for 5 minutes. Remove from the heat. Sift the flour
into a bowl, then add the hazelnuts. Rub in the butter, then sift in
the remaining superfine sugar. Add the lemon rind, egg yolk, and
3 tablespoons of the milk and mix. Knead briefly on a lightly floured
counter, then let rest for 30 minutes.

Preheat the oven to 375°F/190°C. Grease an 8-inch/20-cm ovenproof pie
dish. Roll out half the dough to a thickness of ¹/₄ inch/5 mm and use to line
the dish. Spoon the fruit into the pastry shell. Brush the rim with water,
then roll out the remaining dough and use it to cover the pie. Trim and
crimp round the edges, make 2 small slits in the top, and decorate with
2 leaf shapes cut from the dough trimmings. Brush all over with the
remaining milk. Bake for 40 minutes. Remove from the oven, sprinkle over
the confectioners' sugar, and serve with whipped cream.

apricot *crumble*

INGREDIENTS

4¹/₂ oz/125 g butter, plus extra
for greasing
scant ⁷/₈ cup packed brown sugar
1 lb 2 oz/500 g fresh apricots, pitted
and sliced
1 tsp ground cinnamon
scant 1¹/₃ cups all-purpose whole-wheat flour
generous ³/₈ cup shelled hazelnuts, toasted
and finely chopped
clotted cream, to serve

SERVES 4

Preheat the oven to 400°F/200°C. Grease a 5-cup ovenproof dish.

Put 3 tablespoons of the butter and scant ¹/₂ cup of the sugar into a pan and melt together, stirring, over low heat. Add the apricots and cinnamon, cover, and let simmer for 5 minutes.

Meanwhile, put the flour into a bowl and rub in the remaining butter. Stir in the remaining sugar, then the hazelnuts. Remove the fruit from the heat and arrange in the bottom of the prepared dish. Sprinkle the crumble topping evenly over the fruit until it is covered all over. Transfer to the oven and bake for 25 minutes, or until the topping is golden. Remove from the oven and serve with clotted cream.

rainy days:

blues

chasers

scotch *broth*

INGREDIENTS

1 large onion, quartered
6 lamb shanks, weighing about
3 lb 8 oz/1.6 kg
1 whole garlic bulb, unpeeled,
the outer loose layers removed
4 unsmoked bacon slices, diced
1 tbsp vegetable oil
1 large onion, diced
3 carrots, sliced
1 small rutabaga, cut into chunks
1 small celeriac, cut into chunks
3 leeks, halved lengthwise and
thickly sliced
3 fresh thyme sprigs
1 fresh bay leaf
1 tsp salt
1 tsp pepper
$3^{1}/_{2}$ cups chicken or beef stock
scant $^{1}/_{3}$ cup pearl barley
4 tbsp chopped fresh parsley

SERVES 6

Preheat the oven to 450°F/230°C. Roast the quartered onion, lamb, and garlic in a roasting pan for 30 minutes, or until well browned, turning occasionally. Turn into a large heavy-bottom pan. Pour over water to cover. Slowly bring to a boil, skimming off any foam. Cook over low heat, partially covered, for $1^{1}/_{4}$ hours.

Meanwhile, crisp the bacon in the oil in a separate large pan. Add the diced onion, vegetables, herbs, salt, and pepper. Pour over the stock and add the barley. Bring to a boil, then reduce the heat, cover, and let simmer for 35–40 minutes.

Remove the lamb and garlic from the first pan with a slotted spoon. Strip the meat from the bones and squeeze out the garlic pulp. Line a strainer with paper towels. Strain the lamb cooking liquid into a bowl. Blot up any surface fat with paper towels. Add 3 cups of the strained liquid, with the meat and garlic pulp, to the vegetables in the other pan. Bring to a boil, then let simmer for 10 minutes.

Stir in the parsley just before serving.

INGREDIENTS

generous 1 cup red split lentils
6$^{1/3}$ cups vegetable stock
1 garlic clove, chopped
1 onion, chopped
1 leek, chopped
1 large carrot, chopped
5 tomatoes, peeled and chopped
1 bay leaf
salt and pepper
6 oz/175 g potatoes, chopped

2$^{3/4}$ oz/75 g sweet potato, chopped
5$^{1/2}$ oz/150 g smoked ham, diced
pinch of freshly grated nutmeg

TO GARNISH
4 tbsp sour cream
paprika

fresh crusty bread, to serve

ham & lentil *soup*

SERVES 4

Put the lentils into a large pan, pour in the stock, and let soak for 2 hours. Add the garlic, onion, leek, carrot, tomatoes, and bay leaf and season to taste with salt and pepper. Bring to a boil, then reduce the heat, cover, and let simmer for 1 hour, stirring occasionally.

Add all the potatoes with the ham, re-cover and let simmer for an additional 25 minutes, or until the potatoes are tender.

Remove and discard the bay leaf. Transfer half the soup to a food processor and process for 1 minute, or until smooth. Return the mixture to the pan containing the rest of the soup, add the nutmeg, and adjust the seasoning to taste, then reheat gently until warmed through. Ladle into bowls, garnish with a spoonful of sour cream, and sprinkle over a little paprika. Serve with fresh crusty bread.

INGREDIENTS

2 tbsp olive oil
1 onion, chopped
1 garlic clove, chopped
1 tbsp chopped fresh gingerroot
1 small fresh red chili, seeded and
  finely chopped
2 tbsp chopped fresh cilantro
1 bay leaf

2 lb 4 oz/1 kg pumpkin, seeded
  and diced
2$^{1}/_{2}$ cups vegetable stock
salt and pepper
light cream, to garnish

spiced pumpkin *soup*

SERVES 4

Heat the oil in a pan over medium heat. Add the onion and garlic and
cook, stirring, for 4 minutes, or until slightly softened. Add the ginger,
chili, cilantro, bay leaf, and pumpkin and cook for an additional
3 minutes.

Pour in the stock and bring to a boil. Using a slotted spoon, skim any
scum from the surface. Reduce the heat and let simmer gently, stirring
occasionally, for 25 minutes, or until the pumpkin is tender. Remove from
the heat, discard the bay leaf, and let cool slightly.

Transfer the soup to a food processor and blend until smooth (you may
have to do this in batches). Return the soup to the pan and season to taste
with salt and pepper. Reheat gently, stirring. Remove from the heat and
pour into 4 warmed soup bowls. Garnish each one with a swirl of cream
and serve.

winter *minestrone* with sausage

INGREDIENTS

3 tbsp olive oil
9 oz/250 g coarse-textured pork sausage, skinned and cut into chunks
1 onion, thinly sliced
2 garlic cloves, minced
1 cup canned chopped tomatoes
2 tbsp chopped fresh mixed herbs, such as flat-leaf parsley, sage, and marjoram
1 celery stalk, thinly sliced
1 carrot, diced
1 small red bell pepper, seeded and diced
3$^{1}/_{2}$ cups chicken stock
salt and pepper
$^{1}/_{2}$ cup dried short macaroni
$^{1}/_{2}$ cup canned, drained great Northern beans
1 cup frozen peas
2 tbsp freshly grated Parmesan cheese, plus extra to serve
4 thick slices ciabatta or French bread, to serve

SERVES 4

Heat the oil in a large pan over medium–low heat. Add the sausage and onion and cook, stirring occasionally, until the onion is just colored.

Add the garlic, tomatoes, and herbs and cook for 5 minutes, stirring. Add the celery, carrot, and bell pepper, cover, and cook for 5 minutes.

Pour in the stock. Bring to a boil, then reduce the heat, cover, and let simmer gently for 30 minutes.

Season to taste with salt and pepper. Add the macaroni and beans and simmer for 15 minutes, or until the macaroni is just tender.

Stir in the peas and cook for an additional 5 minutes. Stir in the Parmesan cheese.

To serve, place the bread in individual serving bowls. Ladle the soup over the bread and let stand for a few minutes. Serve with plenty of extra Parmesan cheese.

INGREDIENTS

1 lb/450 g potatoes
2 tbsp corn oil
salt and pepper

home-made oven *fries*

SERVES 4

Preheat the oven to 400°F/200°C.

Cut the potatoes into thick, even-size french fries. Rinse them under cold running water and then dry well on a clean dish towel. Put in a bowl, add the oil, and toss together until coated.

Spread the fries on a baking sheet and cook in the oven for 40–45 minutes, turning once, until golden. Add salt and pepper to taste and serve hot.

2 whole garlic bulbs
1 tbsp olive oil
2 lb/900 g mealy potatoes
salt and pepper
$^1/_2$ cup milk
2 oz/55 g butter
fresh parsley sprigs, to garnish

roasted garlic mashed *potatoes*

SERVES 4

Preheat the oven to 350°F/180°C.

Separate the garlic cloves but do not peel, place on a large piece of foil, and drizzle with the oil. Wrap the garlic in the foil and roast in the oven for 1 hour, or until very tender. Let cool slightly.

20 minutes before the end of the cooking time, cut the potatoes into chunks, then cook in a pan of lightly salted water for 15 minutes, or until tender.

Meanwhile, squeeze the cooled garlic cloves out of their skins and push through a strainer into a separate pan. Add the milk and butter. Season to taste with salt and pepper and heat gently until the butter has melted.

Drain the cooked potatoes, then mash in the pan until smooth. Pour in the garlic mixture and heat gently, stirring, until the ingredients are combined. Garnish with parsley sprigs and serve hot.

INGREDIENTS

2 tbsp vegetable oil

4 skinless, boneless chicken breasts, cubed

8 oz/225 g coarse-textured pork sausage, cut into large chunks

4 frankfurters, halved

1 onion, finely chopped

3 carrots, finely sliced

1 garlic clove, minced

1 tsp dried thyme

$^1/_4$–$^1/_2$ tsp dried red pepper flakes

14 oz/400 g canned chopped tomatoes

14 oz/400 g canned cannellini beans, drained and rinsed

$^2/_3$ cup chicken stock

salt and pepper

chopped fresh flat-leaf parsley, to garnish

chicken, sausage & bean *stew*

SERVES 4

Heat the oil in a large heavy-bottom pan over medium–high heat. Cook the chicken, sausage, and frankfurters until lightly browned. Reduce the heat to medium. Add the onion and carrots and cook for 5 minutes, or until soft.

Stir in the garlic, thyme, and red pepper flakes. Cook for 1 minute. Add the tomatoes, beans, and stock and season to taste with salt and pepper. Bring to a boil, then let simmer over low heat for 20–30 minutes, stirring occasionally.

Garnish with parsley just before serving.

INGREDIENTS

2 tbsp olive oil

6 oz/175 g piece unsmoked bacon,
  sliced into thin strips

3 lb/1.3 kg stewing beef, cut into
  2-inch/5-cm pieces

2 carrots, sliced

2 onions, chopped

2 garlic cloves, very finely chopped

3 tbsp all-purpose flour

3 cups red wine

1^1/$_2$–2 cups beef stock

bouquet garni sachet

1 tsp salt

^{1}/$_2$ tsp pepper

3 tbsp butter

12 oz/350 g pearl onions

12 oz/350 g white mushrooms

2 tbsp chopped fresh parsley, to serve

beef *bourguignon*

SERVES 6

Heat the oil in a large ovenproof casserole, add the bacon, and lightly
brown. Remove with a slotted spoon. Brown the beef, in batches, in the
casserole, drain, and set aside with the bacon. Add the carrots and chopped
onions to the casserole and cook for 5 minutes, or until softened. Add the
garlic and cook until just colored. Return the meat and bacon to the
casserole. Sprinkle over the flour and cook for 1 minute, stirring. Add the
wine and enough stock to cover, the bouquet garni, salt and pepper. Bring
to a boil, then reduce the heat, cover, and let simmer gently for 3 hours.

Heat half the butter in a skillet. Add the pearl onions, cover, and cook until
soft. Remove with a slotted spoon and keep warm. Add the remaining
butter to the skillet and cook the mushrooms. Remove and keep warm.

Strain the casserole liquid into a pan. Wipe the casserole and tip in the
meat, bacon, mushrooms, and onions. Remove the surface fat from the
cooking liquid and let simmer for 1–2 minutes to reduce. Pour over the
meat and vegetables. Serve sprinkled with parsley.

beef pot *roast* with potatoes & dill

INGREDIENTS

2¹/₂ tbsp all-purpose flour

1 tsp salt

¹/₄ tsp pepper

3 lb 8 oz/1.6 kg rolled brisket

2 tbsp vegetable oil

2 tbsp butter

1 onion, finely chopped

2 celery stalks, diced

2 carrots, diced

1 tsp dill seed

1 tsp dried thyme or oregano

1¹/₂ cups red wine

²/₃–1 cup beef stock

4–5 potatoes, cut into large chunks and boiled until just tender

fresh dill sprigs, to serve

SERVES 6

Preheat the oven to 275°F/140°C. Mix 2 tablespoons of the flour with the salt and pepper in a shallow dish. Dip the meat in the seasoned flour to coat. Heat the oil in an ovenproof casserole and brown the meat all over. Transfer to a plate. Heat half the butter in the casserole, add the onion, celery, carrots, dill seed, and thyme and cook for 5 minutes. Return the meat and juices to the casserole.

Pour in the wine and enough stock to reach one-third of the way up the meat. Bring to a boil and cover. Transfer to the oven and cook for 3 hours, turning every 30 minutes. After 2 hours, add the potatoes and more stock if needed.

When ready, transfer the meat and vegetables to a warmed serving dish. Strain the cooking liquid into a pan.

Mix the remaining butter and flour to a paste. Bring the cooking liquid to a boil. Whisk in small pieces of the flour/butter paste, continuing to whisk until the sauce is smooth. Pour the sauce over the meat and vegetables. Sprinkle with dill sprigs and serve.

INGREDIENTS

1 cup dried chickpeas, soaked

3 tbsp vegetable oil

1/2 tsp cumin seeds

1/2 tsp mustard seeds

1 onion, finely chopped

2 garlic cloves, minced

3/4-inch/2-cm piece fresh gingerroot,
   very finely chopped

1 tsp salt

2 tsp ground coriander

1 tsp turmeric

1/2 tsp cayenne pepper

2 tbsp tomato paste

14 oz/400 g canned chopped tomatoes

2 potatoes, cubed

3 tbsp chopped fresh cilantro

1 tbsp lemon juice

generous 1–1 1/4 cups chicken or
   vegetable stock

thinly sliced white or red onion
   rings, to garnish

freshly cooked rice, to serve

chickpea *&* potato *curry*

SERVES 6

Boil the chickpeas rapidly in plenty of water for 15 minutes. Reduce the
heat and boil gently for 1 hour, or until tender. Drain and set aside.

Heat the oil in a large pan or high-sided skillet. Stirring all the time, add
the cumin and mustard seeds, cover, and cook for a few seconds, or until
the seeds pop. Add the onion, cover, and cook for 3–5 minutes, or until just
brown. Add the garlic and ginger and cook for a few seconds. Stir in the
salt, ground coriander, turmeric, and cayenne, then the tomato paste and
tomatoes. Let simmer for a few minutes. Add the chickpeas, potatoes, and
2 tablespoons of the fresh cilantro.

Stir in the lemon juice and generous 1 cup of the stock. Bring to a boil,
then reduce the heat, cover, and let simmer for 30–40 minutes, or until the
potatoes are cooked. Add the extra stock if the mixture becomes too dry.

Serve on a bed of rice, garnished with onion rings and the remaining
fresh cilantro.

INGREDIENTS

4¼ oz/120 g butter, softened, plus
    extra for greasing
scant ⅝ cup packed brown sugar
2 eggs
generous ½ cup all-purpose flour
½ tsp baking powder
2 tbsp unsweetened cocoa
scant ¾ cup blueberries, plus extra
    to decorate

RUM SYRUP
4¼ oz/120 g semisweet chocolate,
    chopped
2 tbsp maple syrup
1 tbsp unsalted butter
1 tbsp rum

blueberry *chocolate*
pudding with rum syrup

SERVES 4

Grease a large ovenproof bowl. Heat water to a depth of 3–4 inches/
7.5–10 cm in a large pan over low heat until simmering.

Put the butter, sugar, eggs, flour, baking powder, and unsweetened cocoa
into a large bowl and beat together until thoroughly mixed. Stir in
the blueberries. Spoon the mixture into the prepared bowl and cover
tightly with 2 layers of foil. Carefully place the bowl in the pan of
simmering water, ensuring that the water level is comfortably lower
than the bowl's rim. Steam the pudding for 1 hour, topping up with
boiling water when necessary.

About 5 minutes before the end of the cooking time, heat the ingredients
for the rum syrup in a small pan over low heat, stirring, until smooth and
melted. Remove the pudding from the heat, discard the foil, and run a
knife around the edge to loosen the pudding. Turn out onto a serving dish,
pour over the syrup, and decorate with blueberries. Serve at once.

jam *roly-poly*

scant 1¹/₄ cups self-rising flour, plus extra
for dusting
pinch of salt
scant ³/₄ cup shredded suet
3–4 tbsp hot water
6 tbsp raspberry preserves
2 tbsp milk
1 tbsp butter, for greasing
fresh raspberries, to decorate
hot stirred custard, to serve

SERVES 4

Put the flour and salt into a bowl and mix together well. Add the suet, then stir in enough of the hot water to make a light dough. Using your hands, shape the dough into a ball. Turn out the dough onto a lightly floured counter and knead gently until smooth. Roll out into a rectangle about 11 x 9 inches/ 28 x 23 cm.

Spread the preserves over the dough, leaving a border of about ¹/₂ inch/1 cm all round. Brush the border with milk. Starting with the short side, roll up the dough evenly until you have one large roll.

Lightly grease a large piece of foil, then place the dough roll in the center. Gently close up the foil around the dough, allowing room for expansion, and seal tightly. Transfer to a steamer set over a pan of boiling water. Steam for 1¹/₂ hours, or until cooked, topping up the water level when necessary.

Turn out the roly-poly onto a serving platter and decorate with raspberries. Serve with hot stirred custard.

INGREDIENTS

1 tbsp butter, for greasing
1/2 cup golden raisins
5 tbsp superfine sugar
scant 1/2 cup pudding rice
5 cups milk
1 tsp vanilla extract
finely grated rind of 1 large lemon
pinch of freshly grated nutmeg
chopped pistachios, to decorate

creamy rice *pudding*

SERVES 4

Preheat the oven to 325°F/160°C. Grease a 3^{1}/$_{2}$-cup ovenproof dish
with butter.

Put the golden raisins, sugar, and rice into a mixing bowl, then stir in the
milk and vanilla extract. Transfer to the prepared dish, sprinkle over the
lemon rind and the nutmeg, then bake in the oven for 2^{1}/$_{2}$ hours.

Remove from the oven and transfer to individual serving bowls. Decorate
with chopped pistachios and serve.

INGREDIENTS

PUDDING
scant 1/2 cup golden raisins
scant 1 cup pitted dates, chopped
1 tsp baking soda
2 tbsp butter, plus extra for greasing
scant 1 cup packed brown sugar
2 eggs
scant 1 1/3 cups self-rising flour, sifted

STICKY TOFFEE SAUCE
2 tbsp butter
3/4 cup heavy cream
scant 1 cup packed brown sugar
thin strips of orange zest, to decorate
whipped cream, to serve

sticky toffee *pudding*

SERVES 4

Preheat the oven to 350°F/180°C. Grease an 8-inch/20-cm round cake pan.

To make the pudding, put the fruit and baking soda into a heatproof bowl. Cover with boiling water and let soak. Put the butter in a separate bowl, add the sugar, and mix well. Beat in the eggs, then fold in the flour. Drain the soaked fruit, add to the bowl, and mix. Spoon the mixture evenly into the prepared cake pan. Transfer to the oven and bake for 35–40 minutes. The pudding is cooked when a skewer inserted into the center comes out clean.

About 5 minutes before the end of the cooking time, make the sauce. Melt the butter in a pan over medium heat. Stir in the cream and sugar and bring to a boil, stirring constantly. Reduce the heat and let simmer for 5 minutes.

Turn out the pudding onto a serving plate and pour over the sauce. Decorate with strips of orange zest and serve with whipped cream.

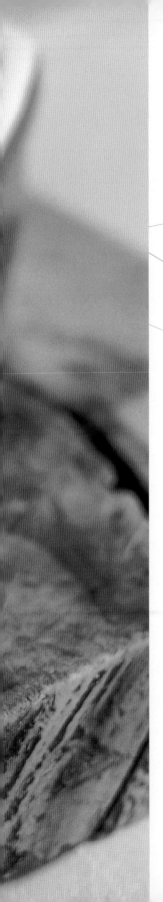

CHAPTER 3

lazy

weekends

2 lb/900 g mealy potatoes
salt and pepper
4 skinless, boneless chicken breasts
2 tbsp vegetable oil
1 onion, finely chopped
1 garlic clove, finely chopped
2 tbsp chopped fresh parsley
4 eggs

chicken *hash* with fried *eggs*

SERVES 4

Cut the potatoes into 3/4-inch/2-cm dice and cook in a large pan of lightly salted water for 5 minutes, or until just tender. Drain well.

Cut the chicken into 3/4-inch/2-cm pieces. Heat half the oil in a large skillet. Add the onion and garlic and cook, stirring, for 5 minutes, or until the onion has softened. Add the chicken and season to taste with salt and pepper. Cook, stirring, for an additional 5 minutes, or until the onion and chicken have browned.

Add the drained potatoes and cook, stirring occasionally, for 10 minutes, or until the potatoes have browned. Stir in the parsley.

Meanwhile, in a separate skillet, heat the remaining oil. Break the eggs individually into the hot oil and cook until set.

Divide the chicken hash between individual serving plates and top each serving with a fried egg.

INGREDIENTS

1 lb/450 g potatoes
1 egg, beaten
4 tbsp all-purpose flour, plus extra
  for dusting
salt and pepper
1 lb/450 g sliced lambs' liver
corn oil, for pan-frying
4 bacon slices
2 onions, finely sliced
fresh parsley sprigs, to garnish

pan-fried liver & bacon with potato *cakes*

SERVES 4

Grate the potatoes, then rinse under cold running water until the water runs clear. Squeeze out the water and dry the potatoes in a clean dish towel. Put the potatoes into a large bowl and add the egg and flour, then season to taste with salt and pepper and mix well together.

Dust the liver with flour and season to taste with salt and pepper.

Heat about 1/4 inch/5 mm oil in a large skillet, then add large tablespoons of the potato mixture, flattening them with a spatula. Cook, turning once, for 10 minutes, or until golden brown. Remove from the skillet and keep hot. Continue until all the mixture has been cooked.

Meanwhile, in a separate skillet, heat enough oil to cover the bottom. Add the bacon and cook until crisp, then push to one side of the skillet. Add the onions and cook for 5 minutes, or until browned. Push to one side of the pan, add the liver, and cook, turning once, for 6–8 minutes, or until tender. Serve with the potato cakes, garnished with parsley sprigs.

salisbury *steak*

1 tbsp vegetable oil
1 small onion, thinly sliced
4 white mushrooms, thinly sliced
$1/2$ cup fresh ground beef
salt and pepper
$1/4$ ciabatta loaf
1 tomato, sliced (optional)
$1/4$ cup red wine or beef stock

SERVES 1

Heat the oil in a small skillet over high heat. Add the onion and mushrooms and cook quickly until soft. Push the vegetables to the side of the skillet.

Season the beef to taste with salt and pepper, then shape into a round patty. Add to the skillet and cook until starting to brown, then carefully flip over and cook the second side.

Slice the ciabatta horizontally through the center, toast lightly, and arrange on a serving dish. Top with the tomato slices, if using.

Remove the meat patty from the skillet and set it on the ciabatta.

Bring the onions and mushrooms back to the center of the skillet, pour over the wine, and heat until boiling. Continue boiling for 1 minute, or until slightly reduced, then remove from the heat and spoon over the meat patty. Serve at once.

INGREDIENTS

1 lb/450 g frozen spinach, thawed
salt and pepper
1 lb/450 g ricotta cheese
8 sheets no-precook lasagna
scant 2¹/₂ cups strained tomatoes
8 oz/225 g mozzarella cheese,
  thinly sliced
1 tbsp freshly grated Parmesan cheese
fresh salad, to serve (optional)

cheese & spinach *lasagna*

SERVES 4

Preheat the oven to 350°F/180°C.

Put the spinach in a strainer and squeeze out any excess liquid. Put half in the bottom of an ovenproof dish and season to taste with salt and pepper.

Spread half the ricotta over the spinach, cover with half the lasagna sheets, then spoon over half the strained tomatoes. Arrange half the mozzarella cheese slices on top. Repeat the layers and finally sprinkle over the Parmesan cheese.

Bake in the oven for 45–50 minutes, or until the top is brown and bubbling.

Serve with salad, if desired.

INGREDIENTS

12 oz/350 g haddock fillets

12 oz/350 g halibut fillets

12 oz/350 g salmon fillets

2^1/$_2$ cups milk

^{1}/$_2$ cup brandy

2 lb 4 oz/1 kg potatoes, sliced

salt and pepper

5 tbsp butter, plus extra for greasing

3 tbsp all-purpose flour

1 tbsp chopped fresh parsley

1 tbsp chopped fresh cilantro

2 onions, 1 grated and 1 sliced

3 oz/85 g Cheddar cheese, grated

selection of freshly cooked
   vegetables, to serve

mixed fish & potato *pie*

SERVES 4

Preheat the oven to 400°F/200°C. Rinse all the fish, then pat dry with paper towels. Pour the milk into a pan and bring to a boil. Add the haddock and halibut and cook gently for 10 minutes. Lift out and set aside. Reserve the milk. In a separate pan, cook the salmon in the brandy over low heat for 10 minutes. Lift out and set aside. Reserve the cooking liquid. Cut all the fish into small chunks.

Cook the potatoes in a large pan of lightly salted water for 15 minutes. Meanwhile, in a separate small pan, melt the butter over low heat, stir in the flour, and cook for 1 minute. Stir in the reserved milk and brandy liquid to make a smooth sauce. Bring to a boil, then reduce the heat and let simmer for 10 minutes. Remove from the heat and stir in the herbs. Drain and mash the potatoes, then add the grated onion. Season to taste with salt and pepper. Grease a large pie dish, then add the fish. Top with the sliced onion. Pour over enough sauce to cover. Top with the mashed potato, then the cheese. Bake for 30 minutes. Serve with vegetables.

moussaka

2 eggplants, thinly sliced
1 lb/450 g fresh lean ground beef
2 onions, finely sliced
1 tsp finely chopped garlic
14 oz/400 g canned tomatoes
2 tbsp chopped fresh parsley
salt and pepper
2 eggs
1¼ cups lowfat plain yogurt
1 tbsp freshly grated Parmesan cheese

SERVES 4

In a large nonstick skillet, dry-fry the eggplant slices, in batches, on both sides until brown. Remove from the skillet.

Add the beef to the skillet and cook for 5 minutes, stirring, until browned. Stir in the onions and garlic and cook for 5 minutes, or until lightly browned. Add the tomatoes and parsley and season to taste with salt and pepper. Bring the mixture to a boil, then reduce the heat and let simmer for 20 minutes, or until the meat is tender.

Preheat the oven to 350°F/180°C. Arrange half the eggplant slices in a layer in an ovenproof dish. Add the meat mixture, then a final layer of the remaining eggplant slices.

In a bowl, beat the eggs, then beat in the yogurt and add salt and pepper to taste. Pour the mixture over the eggplant and sprinkle the cheese on top. Bake the moussaka in the oven for 45 minutes, or until golden brown. Serve straight from the dish.

INGREDIENTS

2 tbsp olive oil

8 oz/225 g coarse-textured pure
   pork sausage, skinned and cut
   into chunks

2 onions, finely chopped

4 carrots, thickly sliced

6 potatoes, cut into chunks

2 large garlic cloves, minced

2 tsp chopped fresh rosemary

2 tsp chopped fresh thyme or oregano

2 lb 10 oz/1.2 kg canned
   chopped tomatoes

salt and pepper

2 tbsp chopped fresh flat-leaf
   parsley, to garnish

sausage & tomato *pot*

SERVES 4

Heat the oil in a large heavy-bottom pan over medium–high heat. Add the sausage and cook until browned. Remove from the pan with a slotted spoon and set aside.

Reduce the heat to medium. Add the onions, carrots, potatoes, garlic, rosemary, and thyme to the pan. Cover and cook gently for 10 minutes, stirring occasionally.

Return the sausage to the pan. Pour in the tomatoes and bring to a boil. Season to taste with salt and pepper. Cover and let simmer over medium–low heat, stirring occasionally, for 45 minutes, or until the vegetables are tender.

Sprinkle with the parsley just before serving.

INGREDIENTS

2 tbsp vegetable oil

1 lb/450 g skinless, boneless
chicken breasts, cubed

1 onion, finely chopped

1 green bell pepper, seeded and
finely chopped

1 potato, diced

1 sweet potato, diced

2 garlic cloves, minced

1–2 fresh green chilies, seeded and
very finely chopped

7 oz/200 g canned chopped tomatoes

$\frac{1}{2}$ tsp dried oregano

$\frac{1}{2}$ tsp salt

$\frac{1}{4}$ tsp pepper

4 tbsp chopped fresh cilantro

2 cups chicken stock

mexican chicken, chili & potato *pot*

SERVES 4

Heat the oil in a large heavy-bottom pan over medium–high heat. Add the chicken and cook until lightly browned.

Reduce the heat to medium. Add the onion, bell pepper, potato, and sweet potato. Cover and cook, stirring occasionally, for 5 minutes, or until the vegetables start to soften.

Add the garlic and chilies and cook for 1 minute. Stir in the tomatoes, oregano, salt, pepper, and half the cilantro and cook for 1 minute.

Pour in the stock. Bring to a boil, then cover and let simmer over medium–low heat for 15–20 minutes, or until the chicken is cooked through and the vegetables are tender.

Sprinkle with the remaining cilantro just before serving.

lamb, garlic & bean *casserole*

INGREDIENTS

2 tbsp olive oil, plus extra for drizzling
2 lb/900 g boneless lamb, cut into
1¹/₂-inch/4-cm cubes
2 onions, finely chopped
1 tbsp chopped fresh rosemary
12 large garlic cloves, peeled and left whole
2–3 anchovy fillets, coarsely chopped
2 tbsp all-purpose flour
¹/₂ tsp pepper
2¹/₂ cups chicken or lamb stock
1¹/₃ cups dried cannellini or Great Northern
beans, soaked overnight and drained
salt
1 cup stale, coarse bread crumbs
chopped fresh flat-leaf parsley,
to garnish

SERVES 4

Preheat the oven to 300°F/150°C. Heat half the oil in an ovenproof casserole. When very hot, cook the lamb, in batches, until evenly browned. Remove with a slotted spoon and transfer to a plate. Cook the onions and rosemary in the remaining oil in the casserole, stirring, for 5–7 minutes, or until golden brown. Reduce the heat, stir in the garlic and anchovies, and cook for 1 minute.

Return the meat and any juices to the casserole. Sprinkle with the flour and stir well. Season with the pepper. Pour in the stock, stirring constantly, and add the drained beans.

Bring to a boil, cover tightly, and cook in the oven for 2 hours, or until soft. Remove from the oven. Season to taste with salt.

Preheat the broiler to high. Spread the bread crumbs over the lamb and beans. Drizzle a little oil over the top. Place under the broiler for a few minutes, or until the crumbs are golden brown. Sprinkle with parsley and serve at once.

INGREDIENTS

3 tbsp vegetable oil
1 lb/450 g fresh ground beef
1 onion, finely chopped
1 green bell pepper, seeded and diced
2 garlic cloves, minced
1 lb 12 oz/800 g canned
  chopped tomatoes
14 oz/400 g canned red kidney beans,
  drained and rinsed
1 tsp ground cumin

1 tsp salt
1 tsp sugar
1–3 tsp chili powder
2 tbsp chopped fresh cilantro

speedy *chili* beef

SERVES 4

Heat the oil in a large ovenproof casserole over medium–high heat. Add the beef and cook, stirring, until lightly browned.

Reduce the heat to medium. Add the onion, bell pepper, and garlic and cook for 5 minutes, or until soft.

Stir in the remaining ingredients, except the cilantro. Bring to a boil, then let simmer over medium–low heat, stirring frequently, for 30 minutes.

Stir in the cilantro just before serving.

INGREDIENTS

4 tbsp all-purpose flour

salt and pepper

1/4 cup olive oil

8 pieces neck of lamb or lamb chops

1 green bell pepper, seeded and
  thinly sliced

1–2 fresh green chilies,
  seeded and thinly sliced

1 small onion, thinly sliced

2 garlic cloves, thinly sliced

2 tbsp fresh basil, coarsely torn

1/2 cup red wine

4 tbsp red wine vinegar

8 cherry tomatoes

1/2 cup water

1 quantity Basic Risotto
  (see page 13), made with
  beef stock and red wine

hot pepper lamb
in red wine *risotto*

SERVES 4

Mix the flour with salt and pepper to taste on a plate. Heat the oil in a
skillet large enough to take all the lamb in a single layer over high heat.
Dredge the lamb in the seasoned flour, shaking off any excess. Brown the
lamb in the skillet, remove with a slotted spoon, and set aside.

Toss the bell pepper, chilies, onion, garlic, and basil in the oil left in the
skillet for 3 minutes, or until lightly browned. Add the wine and vinegar,
bring to a boil, and continue cooking over high heat for 3–4 minutes, or
until reduced to 2 tablespoons.

Add the tomatoes and water to the skillet, stir, and bring to a boil.
Return the meat, cover, and reduce the heat as low as possible. Cook for
30 minutes, or until the meat is tender, turning occasionally. Check
regularly and add 2–3 tablespoons of water if necessary. Meanwhile,
prepare the Basic Risotto as on page 13. Arrange a scoop of risotto on each
plate and sprinkle with some bell peppers and tomatoes. Arrange the lamb
on top and serve.

baked pears
with chocolate *custard*

INGREDIENTS

4 ripe pears
1 tbsp lime juice
2 tbsp red wine
2 oz/55 g butter
4 tbsp brown sugar
1 tsp allspice

CHOCOLATE CUSTARD
1 heaping tbsp custard powder
1 tbsp cornstarch
1 tbsp unsweetened cocoa
1 tbsp brown sugar
generous 1 cup milk
1¹/₂ cups light cream
2 tbsp grated semisweet chocolate

thin strips of lime zest, to decorate

SERVES 4

Preheat the oven to 400°F/200°C. Peel and core the pears, leaving them whole, then brush with lime juice. Put the pears into a small, nonstick baking pan, then pour over the wine.

Heat the butter, sugar, and allspice in a small pan over low heat, stirring, until melted. Pour the mixture over the pears. Bake in the oven, basting occasionally, for 25 minutes, or until golden and cooked through.

About 5 minutes before the end of the cooking time, heat the custard powder, cornstarch, unsweetened cocoa, sugar, and milk in a pan over low heat, stirring, until thickened and almost boiling. Remove from the heat, add the cream and grated chocolate, and stir until melted.

Divide the custard between serving dishes. Remove the pears from the oven and put a pear in the center of each pool of custard. Decorate with strips of lime zest and serve.

INGREDIENTS

4 oz/115 g butter, softened, plus extra
 for greasing
scant 1 cup packed brown sugar
2 eggs
3 bananas
scant 1⅝ cups all-purpose flour
1 tsp baking soda
1 tbsp unsweetened cocoa
1 tsp allspice
½ cup thick plain yogurt
½ cup semisweet chocolate chips

chocolate banana *loaf*

SERVES 4–6

Preheat the oven to 350°F/180°C. Grease a 9 x 5 x 3-inch/23 x 13 x 7.5-cm
loaf pan.

Put the butter, sugar, and eggs into a bowl and beat well. Peel and mash the
bananas, then add to the mixture. Stir in well. Sift the flour, baking soda,
unsweetened cocoa, and allspice into a separate bowl, then add to the
banana mixture and mix well. Stir in the yogurt and chocolate chips. Spoon
the mixture into the prepared pan and level the surface.

Bake in the oven for 1 hour. To test whether the loaf is cooked through,
insert a skewer into the center—it should come out clean. If not, return the
loaf to the oven for a few minutes.

INGREDIENTS

3 tbsp butter, plus extra for greasing
2 tbsp superfine sugar
2 eggs
6 tbsp all-purpose flour, sifted
1 tsp baking powder, sifted
6 tbsp milk
1 tsp vanilla extract
4 tbsp corn syrup
thin strips of candied orange peel,
  to decorate
hot stirred custard, to serve

golden *pudding*

SERVES 4–6

Lightly grease a 3½-cup ovenproof bowl. Put the butter into a bowl with
the sugar and cream together until fluffy. Add the eggs and beat together
well. Mix in the flour and baking powder, then stir in the milk and vanilla
extract. Continue to stir until smooth.

Pour the corn syrup into the ovenproof bowl, then spoon the pudding
mixture on top. Cover with waxed paper and top with a piece of
foil, tied on securely with string. Transfer to a large pan filled with enough
simmering water to reach halfway up the sides of the ovenproof bowl. Let
simmer gently for 1½ hours, or until cooked right through, topping up
with boiling water when necessary.

Lift out the pudding and let rest for 5 minutes, then turn it out onto a
serving plate. Decorate with thin strips of candied orange peel and serve
with hot stirred custard.

tiramisù

INGREDIENTS

scant 1 cup strong black coffee, cooled
to room temperature
4 tbsp orange-flavored liqueur,
such as Cointreau
3 tbsp orange juice
16 Italian ladyfingers
1$^{1}/_{8}$ cups mascarpone cheese
1$^{1}/_{4}$ cups heavy cream,
lightly whipped
3 tbsp confectioners' sugar
grated rind of 1 orange
2$^{1}/_{4}$ oz/60 g chocolate, grated

TO DECORATE
chopped toasted almonds
candied orange peel

SERVES 4

Pour the cooled coffee into a pitcher and stir in the liqueur
and orange juice. Put 8 of the ladyfingers in the bottom of a
serving dish, then pour over half the coffee mixture.

Put the mascarpone cheese in a separate bowl with the cream,
sugar, and orange rind and mix together well. Spread half the
mascarpone mixture over the coffee-soaked ladyfingers,
then arrange the remaining ladyfingers on top. Pour over the
remaining coffee mixture and then spread over the remaining
mascarpone mixture. Sprinkle over the chocolate, cover, and let
chill in the refrigerator for at least 2 hours.

Serve decorated with chopped toasted almonds and candied
orange peel.

CHAPTER 4

family *favorites*

INGREDIENTS

1 lb 10 oz/750 g fresh ground beef
1 beef bouillon cube
1 tbsp minced dried onion
2 tbsp water
1/2 cup grated Cheddar cheese
   (optional)

SERVING SUGGESTIONS
4 sesame buns, toasted
tomato ketchup or chili sauce
mustard
pickled cucumbers, thinly sliced
Spanish onion, thinly sliced
large tomato, thinly sliced
lettuce leaves
french fries

burger & french fries

SERVES 4

Place the beef in a large mixing bowl. Crumble the bouillon cube over the
meat, add the dried onion and water, and mix well. Divide the meat into
4 portions, shape each into a ball, then flatten slightly to make a burger
shape of your preferred thickness.

Preheat a stovetop grill pan over high heat. Place the burgers on the pan
and cook for about 5 minutes on each side, depending on how well done
you like your meat and the thickness of the burgers. Press down
occasionally with a spatula during cooking.

To make cheeseburgers, sprinkle the cheese on top of the meat when you
have turned it the first time.

Serve the burgers on toasted buns, with a selection of the accompaniments
suggested above.

INGREDIENTS

1 lb/450 g mealy potatoes, diced
salt and pepper
2 tbsp milk
2 oz/55 g butter, plus extra
   for greasing
8 oz/225 g green cabbage, shredded
8 oz/225 g carrots, thinly sliced
1 onion, chopped
2 oz/55 g Cheddar cheese, grated

bubble &squeak

SERVES 4

Preheat the oven to 375°F/190°C. Cook the potatoes in a pan of lightly
salted water for 10 minutes, or until tender. Drain well and turn into a
large mixing bowl. Mash until smooth. Beat with the milk, half the butter,
and salt and pepper to taste.

Cook the cabbage and carrots separately in lightly salted water for
5 minutes. Drain well. Mix the cabbage into the potatoes.

Melt the remaining butter in a small skillet, add the onion, and cook
over medium heat until soft but not brown.

Spread a layer of mashed potato in the bottom of a greased shallow
ovenproof dish. Layer the onion on top, then the carrots. Repeat to use up
all the ingredients, finishing with a layer of potato.

Sprinkle the cheese on top and bake in the oven for 45 minutes, or until the
top is golden and crusty. Remove from the oven and serve at once.

shepherd's *pie*

INGREDIENTS

2 lb/900 g mealy potatoes
salt and pepper
12 oz/350 g cold roast lamb, ground
1 onion, finely chopped
2 tbsp all-purpose flour
1 tbsp tomato paste
1¼ cups vegetable stock
2 tbsp chopped fresh parsley,
plus extra to garnish
4 tbsp milk
2 tbsp butter

SERVES 4

Preheat the oven to 350°F/180°C.

Cut the potatoes into chunks and cook in a large pan of lightly salted water for 15 minutes, or until tender.

Meanwhile, put the lamb, onion, flour, tomato paste, stock, parsley, and salt and pepper to taste in a bowl and mix together. Turn out the mixture into an ovenproof dish.

Drain the cooked potatoes, then mash in the pan until smooth. Over low heat, beat in the milk, butter, and salt and pepper to taste until well mixed. Spoon on top of the lamb. Mark the top with a fork.

Bake in the oven for 30 minutes, or until golden brown. Garnish with parsley and serve at once.

INGREDIENTS

2 tbsp vegetable oil
1 lb 8 oz/675 g stewing beef, cubed
3 onions, finely chopped
1 green bell pepper, seeded and diced
2 garlic cloves, very finely chopped
2 tbsp tomato paste
2 tbsp all-purpose flour
14 oz/400 g canned chopped tomatoes
generous 1 cup beef stock
1 fresh bay leaf

3 tbsp chopped fresh parsley
1 tbsp paprika
1 tsp salt
¹/₄ tsp pepper

TO SERVE
buttered noodles
sour cream

beef *goulash*

SERVES 4

Heat the oil in an ovenproof casserole over medium–high heat. Add the beef and cook until evenly browned. Remove and transfer to a bowl with a slotted spoon and set aside.

Add the onions and bell pepper to the casserole and cook, stirring occasionally, for 5 minutes, or until soft. Add the garlic and cook until just colored. Stir in the tomato paste and flour. Cook for 1 minute, stirring constantly.

Return the beef to the casserole. Add the remaining ingredients and bring to a boil. Cover and let simmer over low heat for 2¹/₂ hours, stirring occasionally. Add water or more stock if necessary.

Remove the lid and let simmer for 15 minutes, stirring to prevent sticking, until the sauce has thickened and the meat is very tender.

Serve with buttered noodles and a bowl of sour cream.

INGREDIENTS

PIE DOUGH

1³/4 cups all-purpose whole-wheat
  flour, plus extra for dusting
pinch of salt
3¹/2 oz/100 g butter, diced,
  plus extra for greasing
4 tbsp cold water
2 tbsp milk, for glazing

FILLING

2 tbsp butter
1 onion, chopped

4¹/2 oz/125 g potatoes, chopped
3¹/2 oz/100 g carrots, chopped
1 oz/25 g green beans, chopped
generous ¹/3 cup water
2 tbsp canned and drained
  corn kernels
1 tbsp chopped fresh parsley
2¹/4 oz/60 g Cheddar cheese, grated
salt and pepper

fresh mixed salad, to serve

cheese *&* vegetable *pasties*

SERVES 4

To make the pie dough, sift the flour and salt into a large bowl. Rub in the
butter until the mixture resembles bread crumbs. Add the water and mix
to a dough. Cover with plastic wrap. Let chill for 40 minutes.

To make the filling, melt the butter in a large pan over low heat. Add the
onion, potatoes, and carrots and cook, stirring, for 5 minutes. Add the
green beans and water. Bring to a boil, then reduce the heat and let simmer
for 15 minutes. Remove from the heat, drain, rinse under cold running
water, then drain again. Let cool.

Preheat the oven to 400°F/200°C. Grease a baking sheet. Cut the
dough into quarters and roll out on a floured counter into 4 circles about
6 inches/15 cm in diameter. Mix the vegetables with the corn, parsley,
cheese, and salt and pepper to taste. Spoon onto one half of each dough
circle. Brush the edges with water, then fold over and press together.
Transfer to the prepared baking sheet. Brush all over with milk. Bake in
the oven for 30 minutes, or until golden. Serve with a mixed salad.

steak & kidney *pie*

1 lb 9 oz/700 g rump steak, trimmed and cut
into 1¹/₂-inch/4-cm pieces
3 lambs' kidneys, cored and cut into
1-inch/2.5-cm pieces
2 tbsp all-purpose flour,
plus extra for dusting
salt and pepper
3 tbsp vegetable oil
1 onion, coarsely chopped
1 garlic clove, finely chopped
¹/₂ cup red wine
2 cups stock
1 bay leaf
butter, for greasing
14 oz/400 g ready-made puff pastry
1 egg, beaten

SERVES 4–6

Preheat the oven to 325°F/160°C. Put the meat with the flour and seasoning in a plastic bag and shake until coated. Heat the oil in an ovenproof casserole over high heat and brown the meat in batches. Remove with a slotted spoon and keep warm. Sauté the onion and garlic in the casserole for 2–3 minutes until softened. Stir in the wine and scrape the bottom of the casserole to release the sediment. Pour in the stock, stirring constantly, and bring to a boil. Bubble for 2–3 minutes. Add the bay leaf and return the meat to the casserole. Cover and cook in the oven for 1¹/₂–2 hours. Check the seasoning, then remove the bay leaf. Let cool overnight to develop the flavors.

Preheat the oven to 400°F/200°C. Grease a 5-cup pie dish. Roll out the pastry on a lightly floured counter to 2³/₄ inches/7 cm larger than the pie dish. Cut off a 1¹/₄-inch/3-cm strip. Moisten the rim and press the pastry strip onto it. Place a pie funnel in the center of the dish and spoon in the filling. Moisten the pastry collar with water and put on the pastry lid, taking care to fit it around the funnel. Crimp the edges and glaze with the egg. Place on a sheet and cook in the oven for 30 minutes, or until golden brown and the filling bubbling hot.

INGREDIENTS

CAKE

butter, for greasing
scant $^3/_4$ cup self-rising flour
pinch of salt
1 tsp allspice
$^1/_2$ tsp ground nutmeg
generous $^5/_8$ cup packed brown sugar
2 eggs, beaten
5 tbsp corn oil
$4^1/_2$ oz/125 g carrots, grated
1 banana, chopped
2 tbsp chopped toasted mixed nuts

FROSTING

3 tbsp butter, softened
3 tbsp cream cheese
$1^1/_2$ cups confectioners' sugar, sifted
1 tsp orange juice
grated rind of $^1/_2$ orange

walnut halves or pieces, to decorate

carrot *cake*

MAKES 6

Preheat the oven to 375°F/190°C. Grease a 7-inch/18-cm square cake pan
and line with parchment paper. Sift the flour, salt, allspice, and nutmeg into
a bowl. Stir in the brown sugar, then stir in the eggs and oil. Add the
carrots, banana, and mixed nuts and mix together well.

Spoon the batter into the prepared cake pan and level the surface. Transfer
to the oven and bake for 55 minutes, or until golden and just firm to the
touch. Remove from the oven and let cool. When cool enough to handle,
turn out onto a wire rack, and let cool completely.

To make the frosting, put all the ingredients into a bowl and beat together
until creamy. Spread the frosting over the top of the cold cake, then use a
fork to make shallow wavy lines in the frosting. Sprinkle over the walnuts,
cut the cake into bars, and serve.

INGREDIENTS

CAKE

6 oz/175 g butter, softened, plus extra
    for greasing
generous ¾ cup superfine sugar
4 eggs, lightly beaten
scant 1½ cups self-rising flour
1 tbsp unsweetened cocoa
1¾ oz/50 g semisweet chocolate,
    melted (see page 91)
¼ cup slivered almonds

FILLING

1 tbsp butter, melted
3½ oz/100 g semisweet chocolate,
    melted (see page 91)
scant 1¼ cups heavy cream
2 tbsp confectioners' sugar, plus extra
    for dusting

chocolate cream sandwich *cake*

SERVES 4 – 6

Preheat the oven to 375°F/190°C. Grease 2 x 7-inch/18-cm round sandwich
pans and line the bottoms with parchment paper.

Put the butter and superfine sugar into a bowl and cream until pale and
fluffy. Beat in the eggs. Sift the flour and unsweetened cocoa into a separate
bowl, then fold into the mixture. Fold in the chocolate. Spoon evenly into
the prepared pans, level the surfaces, then sprinkle the almonds over one of
the surfaces only. Bake for 35–40 minutes. Remove from the oven and let
cool for 10 minutes. Turn out onto a wire rack, discard the lining paper,
and let cool.

To make the filling, stir the butter into the melted chocolate. In a separate
bowl, whip the cream until soft peaks form and fold into the chocolate
mixture, then stir in the confectioners' sugar. Spread the filling generously
on the cake without the almond topping, then place the almond-topped
cake carefully on top. Let chill in the refrigerator for 1–2 hours, then dust
with confectioners' sugar before serving.

banoffee *pie*

INGREDIENTS

2 x 14 fl oz/400 ml cans sweetened
condensed milk
6 tbsp butter, melted, plus extra
for greasing
5¹/2 oz/150 g graham crackers,
crushed into crumbs
scant ¹/3 cup almonds,
toasted and ground
generous ¹/3 cup shelled hazelnuts,
toasted and ground
4 ripe bananas
1 tbsp lemon juice
1 tsp vanilla extract
2³/4 oz/75 g chocolate, grated
2 cups thick
heavy cream, whipped

SERVES 4

Place the cans of milk in a large pan and cover them with water.
Bring to a boil, then reduce the heat and let simmer for
2 hours. Ensure that the water is topped up regularly to keep the
cans covered. Carefully lift out the hot cans and let cool.

Preheat the oven to 350°F/180°C. Grease a 9-inch/23-cm tart pan.
Put the butter into a bowl and add the graham cracker crumbs
and nuts. Mix together well, then press the mixture evenly into
the bottom and sides of the tart pan. Bake for 10–12 minutes,
then remove from the oven and let cool.

Peel and slice the bananas and put them into a bowl. Sprinkle
over the lemon juice and vanilla extract and mix gently. Spread
the banana mixture over the cookie crust in the pan, then open
the cans of condensed milk and spoon the contents over the
bananas. Sprinkle over 1³/4 oz/50 g of the chocolate, then top with
a thick layer of whipped cream. Sprinkle over the remaining
chocolate and serve.

chocolate chip *muffins*

INGREDIENTS

3^{1}/$_{2}$ oz/100 g butter, softened
scant ^{2}/$_{3}$ cup superfine sugar
scant ^{1}/$_{2}$ cup packed brown sugar
2 eggs
^{2}/$_{3}$ cup sour cream
5 tbsp milk
generous 1^{3}/$_{4}$ cups all-purpose flour
1 tsp baking soda
2 tbsp unsweetened cocoa
generous 1 cup semisweet chocolate chips

MAKES 12

Preheat the oven to 375°F/190°C. Line a 12-cup muffin pan with paper cases.

Put the butter, superfine sugar, and brown sugar into a bowl and beat well. Beat in the eggs, cream, and milk until thoroughly mixed. Sift the flour, baking soda, and unsweetened cocoa into a separate bowl and stir into the mixture. Add the chocolate chips and mix well. Spoon the batter into the paper cases. Bake in the oven for 25–30 minutes.

Remove from the oven and let cool for 10 minutes. Turn out onto a wire rack and let cool completely. Store in an airtight container until required.

INGREDIENTS

3¹/₄ oz/90 g butter or margarine,
  plus extra for greasing
generous ¹/₄ cup packed brown sugar
5 tbsp molasses
1 egg white
1 tsp almond extract
scant 1¹/₄ cups all-purpose flour,
  plus extra for dusting
¹/₄ tsp baking soda

¹/₄ tsp baking powder
pinch of salt
¹/₂ tsp allspice
¹/₂ tsp ground ginger
4¹/₂ oz/125 g eating apples, cooked
  and finely chopped

gingerbread *squares*

MAKES 24

Preheat the oven to 350°F/180°C. Grease a large baking sheet and line it
with parchment paper. Put the butter, sugar, molasses, egg white, and
almond extract into a food processor and blend until smooth.

In a separate bowl, sift the flour, baking soda, baking powder, salt, allspice,
and ginger together. Add to the creamed mixture and beat together
thoroughly. Stir in the chopped apples. Pour the mixture onto the prepared
baking sheet.

Transfer to the oven and bake for 10 minutes, or until golden brown.
Remove from the oven and cut into 24 pieces. Transfer the squares to a
wire rack and let them cool completely before serving.

INGREDIENTS

2¹/2 oz/70 g semisweet chocolate,
  chopped
1 cup all-purpose flour
³/4 tsp baking soda
¹/4 tsp baking powder
8 oz/225 g unsalted butter,
  plus extra for greasing

¹/2 cup raw brown sugar
¹/2 tsp almond extract
1 egg
1 tsp milk
¹/2 cup shelled pecans,
  finely chopped

pecan *brownies*

MAKES 20

Preheat the oven to 350°F/180°C. Grease a large baking sheet and line it
with parchment paper.

Put the chocolate into a heatproof bowl set over a pan of barely simmering
water (a double boiler is ideal) and heat until it is melted. While the
chocolate is melting, sift the flour, baking soda, and baking powder
together into a large bowl.

In a separate bowl, cream the butter and sugar together, then mix in the
almond extract and the egg. Remove the chocolate from the heat and stir
into the butter mixture. Add the flour mixture, milk, and chopped nuts to
the bowl and stir until well combined.

Spoon the batter onto the prepared baking sheet and level it. Transfer to
the oven and bake for 30 minutes, or until firm to the touch (it should
still be a little gooey in the center). Remove from the oven and let cool
completely. Cut into 20 squares and serve.

fruit *crêpes*

INGREDIENTS

CREPES
scant 1 cup all-purpose flour
pinch of salt
2 eggs
1¼ cups milk
2–3 tbsp vegetable oil

FILLING
1 banana
1 tbsp lemon juice
2 nectarines, pitted and
cut into small pieces
1 mango, peeled, pitted, and
cut into small pieces
3 kiwifruit, peeled and
cut into small pieces
2 tbsp maple syrup

confectioners' sugar, for dusting
whipped cream, to serve

SERVES 4

To make the crêpes, sift the flour and salt into a bowl. Whisk in the eggs and milk. Cover with plastic wrap and let chill for 30 minutes.

To make the filling, peel and slice the banana and put into a large bowl. Pour over the lemon juice and stir gently until coated. Add the nectarines, mango, kiwifruit, and maple syrup and stir together gently until mixed.

Heat a little oil in a skillet until hot. Remove the crêpe batter from the refrigerator and add a large spoonful to the skillet. Cook over high heat until golden, then turn over and cook briefly on the other side. Remove from the skillet and keep warm. Cook the other crêpes in the same way, stacking them on a plate. Keep warm. Divide the fruit filling between the crêpes and fold into triangles or roll into horns. Dust with confectioners' sugar and serve with whipped cream.

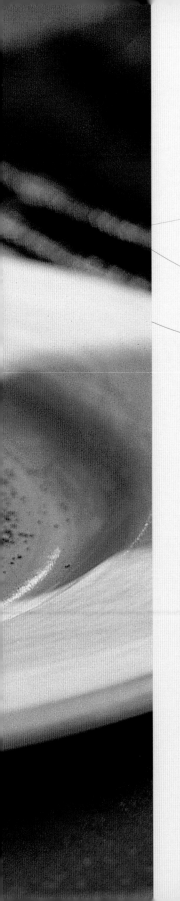

CHAPTER 5

chocolate
desserts

INGREDIENTS

CAKE

butter, for greasing

4¹/₂ oz/125 g semisweet chocolate, chopped

1³/₄ oz/50 g bittersweet chocolate, chopped

3 tbsp warm water

2 tbsp coffee-flavored liqueur, such as Kahlúa (optional)

5 eggs, separated

⁷/₈ cup superfine sugar

FILLING

2 cups heavy cream

generous ³/₈ cup confectioners' sugar, sifted, plus extra for dusting

scant ¹/₄ cup unsweetened cocoa

2 tsp espresso coffee powder, dissolved in 1 tbsp boiling water

halved strawberries, to decorate

rich chocolate *roulade*

SERVES 4–6

Preheat the oven to 350°F/180°C. Grease and line a 14 x 10-inch/35 x 25-cm jelly roll pan.

Put the chocolate into a heatproof bowl and set over a pan of hot water, stirring occasionally, until melted. Stir in the water and liqueur, if using. Whisk the egg yolks and superfine sugar in a separate bowl until pale. Beat the chocolate into the yolk mixture. Whisk the egg whites in another bowl until stiff, then fold into the chocolate mixture. Pour into the prepared pan and bake for 15 minutes. Remove, cover with waxed paper, and let cool for 3–4 hours. Meanwhile, whisk all the filling ingredients together in a bowl until thick. Cover with plastic wrap and let chill.

Turn out the cake onto waxed paper dusted with confectioners' sugar. Discard the lining paper. Set aside 4 tablespoons of the filling, then spread the rest over the roulade, leaving a 1-inch/2.5-cm border. Starting from a short side, roll up the cake. Discard the paper. Pipe the remaining filling on top, decorate with strawberries, and serve.

INGREDIENTS

scant 1/2 cup pitted dates, chopped

generous 1/4 cup raisins

generous 1/4 cup golden raisins

1 tsp almond extract

1 1/2 oz/40 g semisweet chocolate, melted (see page 91)

8 slices day-old white or whole-wheat bread, crusts removed

3 eggs

2 tbsp almond-flavored liqueur, such as amaretto

scant 1 1/4 cups milk

3 oz/85 g semisweet chocolate, grated

1/4 cup slivered almonds

1/2 tsp allspice

heavy cream, to serve

chocolate bread *pudding*

SERVES 4

Preheat the oven to 350°F/180°C.

Put the dates, raisins, and golden raisins into a large bowl, pour over the almond extract, and set aside to soak. Spread the melted chocolate evenly over one side of each slice of bread, then cut each slice in half diagonally and then again to make 4 triangles. Arrange half the triangles in a layer in the bottom of an ovenproof dish, then spoon over the fruit with the almond extract. Arrange the remaining bread triangles in a layer over the top.

Put the eggs and liqueur into a heatproof bowl and beat well. Heat the milk and chocolate in a pan over low heat, stirring, until melted and hot, but not boiling. Remove from the heat and stir into the beaten eggs. Pour over the bread pudding, then top with the almonds. Sprinkle over the allspice.

Bake in the oven for 30 minutes, or until risen. Remove from the oven and serve with generous spoonfuls of cream.

chocolate cherry *gâteau*

INGREDIENTS

2 lb/900 g fresh cherries, pitted and halved
scant 1^1/$_3$ cups superfine sugar
generous ^{1}/$_3$ cup cherry brandy
scant ^{3}/$_4$ cup all-purpose flour
^{1}/$_2$ cup unsweetened cocoa
^{1}/$_2$ tsp baking powder
4 eggs
3 tbsp unsalted butter, melted, plus extra,
unmelted, for greasing
4 cups heavy cream

TO DECORATE
grated semisweet chocolate
whole fresh cherries

SERVES 4–6

Preheat the oven to 350°F/180°C. Grease and line a 9-inch/
23-cm springform cake pan. Put the cherries into a pan with
3 tablespoons of the sugar and the cherry brandy. Let simmer for
5 minutes. Drain, reserving the syrup. In a bowl, sift the flour,
unsweetened cocoa, and baking powder together.

Put the eggs into a heatproof bowl and beat in generous ^{3}/$_4$ cup
of the remaining sugar. Place the bowl over a pan of barely
simmering water and beat for 6 minutes, or until thickened.
Remove from the heat, then gradually fold in the flour mixture
and melted butter. Spoon into the prepared cake pan. Bake for
40 minutes. Remove from the oven and let cool. Turn out the
cake and cut in half horizontally.

Whip the cream with the remaining sugar until peaks form.
Spread the reserved syrup over the cut sides of the cake. Arrange
the cherries over one half, top with a layer of cream, and place
the other half on top. Cover the whole cake with cream, press
grated chocolate all over, and decorate with cherries.

INGREDIENTS

BASE
4 oz/115 g graham crackers,
  finely crushed
2 tsp unsweetened cocoa
4 tbsp butter, melted, plus extra,
  unmelted, for greasing

CHOCOLATE LAYER
1 lb 12 oz/800 g mascarpone cheese
scant 2 cups confectioners' sugar,
  sifted

juice of ¹/2 orange
finely grated rind of 1 orange
6 oz/175 g semisweet chocolate,
  melted (see page 91)
2 tbsp brandy

TO DECORATE
Chocolate Leaves (see page 110)
halved kumquats

deep chocolate *cheesecake*

SERVES 4–6

Grease an 8-inch/20-cm loose-bottom cake pan.

To make the base, put the crushed graham crackers, unsweetened cocoa, and melted butter into a large bowl and mix well. Press the crumb mixture evenly over the bottom of the prepared pan.

Put the mascarpone cheese and sugar into a bowl and stir in the orange juice and rind. Add the melted chocolate and brandy and mix together until thoroughly combined. Spread the chocolate mixture evenly over the crumb layer. Cover with plastic wrap and let chill for at least 4 hours.

Remove the cheesecake from the refrigerator, turn out onto a serving platter and decorate with Chocolate Leaves (see page 110) and kumquat halves. Serve at once.

INGREDIENTS

12–16 ladyfingers
4 tbsp cherry brandy
15 oz/425 g canned cherries, drained
2 egg yolks
3 tbsp superfine sugar
2 tbsp cornstarch
1 tbsp unsweetened cocoa
1¹/₂ cups milk

²/₃ cup light cream
5 oz/140 g semisweet chocolate,
  grated
³/₄ cup heavy cream
whole fresh cherries, to decorate

dark chocolate *trifle*

SERVES 4

Break the ladyfingers into small pieces and arrange in the base of a
large glass serving bowl. Pour over the cherry brandy and arrange the
cherries on top.

In a heatproof bowl, beat the egg yolks, then beat in the sugar, cornstarch,
and unsweetened cocoa. Heat the milk and light cream in a pan over low
heat, stirring, until just starting to boil. Remove from the heat, then whisk
into the egg mixture. Return the mixture to a clean pan and cook over low
heat, stirring, until thickened and smooth. Add half the chocolate and stir
until melted. Remove from the heat and let cool to room temperature. Pour
the custard over the cherries, cover with plastic wrap, and let chill for at
least 8 hours or overnight.

Whip the heavy cream in a bowl until peaks form. Spoon a layer over the
trifle, then sprinkle over the remaining chocolate and cherries. Serve
at once, or cover with plastic wrap and let chill until required.

rich chocolate *mousses*

INGREDIENTS

10¹/₂ oz/300 g semisweet chocolate
(at least 70% cocoa solids)
1¹/₂ tbsp unsalted butter
1 tbsp brandy
4 eggs, separated
unsweetened cocoa, for dusting

SERVES 4

Break the chocolate into small pieces and put into a heatproof bowl set over a pan of barely simmering water. Add the butter and melt with the chocolate, stirring, until smooth. Remove from the heat, stir in the brandy, and let cool slightly. Add the egg yolks and beat until smooth.

In a separate bowl, whisk the egg whites until stiff peaks have formed, then fold into the chocolate mixture. Divide 4 stainless steel cooking rings between 4 small serving plates, then spoon the mixture into each ring and level the surfaces. Transfer to the refrigerator and let chill for at least 4 hours until set.

Remove the mousses from the refrigerator and discard the cooking rings. Dust with unsweetened cocoa and serve.

INGREDIENTS

9 oz/250 g semisweet chocolate
  (at least 50% cocoa solids)
generous ¹/₃ cup heavy cream
2 tbsp brandy

SUGGESTED DIPPERS
plain sponge cake, cut into
  bite-size pieces
small pink and white marshmallows
small firm whole fresh fruits, such as
  black currants, blueberries, cherries,
  and strawberries
whole no-soak dried apricots
candied citrus peel,
  cut decoratively into strips
  or bite-size pieces

deep chocolate *fondue*

SERVES 4

Arrange the dippers decoratively on a serving platter or individual serving plates and set aside.

Break or chop the chocolate into small pieces and place in the top of a double boiler or in a heatproof bowl set over a pan of barely simmering water. Pour in the cream and stir until melted and smooth. Stir in the brandy, then carefully pour the mixture into a warmed fondue pot.

Using protective gloves, transfer the fondue pot to a lit tabletop burner. To serve, invite your guests to spear the dippers onto fondue forks and dip them into the fondue.

INGREDIENTS

16 won ton skins
12 oz/350 g semisweet chocolate,
  chopped
1 tbsp cornstarch
3 tbsp cold water
4 cups peanut oil

MAPLE SAUCE
$^3/_4$ cup maple syrup
4 tbsp butter
$^1/_2$ tsp allspice

vanilla ice cream, to serve

chocolate *won tons* with maple sauce

SERVES 4

Spread out the won ton skins on a clean counter, then spoon a little
chopped chocolate into the center of each skin. In a small bowl, mix the
cornstarch and water together until smooth. Brush the edges of the skins
with the cornstarch mixture, then wrap in any preferred shape, such as
triangles, squares, or bundles, and seal the edges. Arrange the won tons on
a serving platter.

To make the maple sauce, put all the ingredients into a pan and stir over
medium heat. Bring to a boil, then reduce the heat and let simmer
for 3 minutes.

Meanwhile, pour the oil into a metal fondue pot (it should be no more than
one-third full). Heat on the stove to 375°F/190°C, or until a cube of bread
browns in 30 seconds. Using protective gloves, transfer the fondue pot to
a lit tabletop burner. To serve, invite your guests to place the won tons on
metal spoons and dip them into the hot oil until cooked (they will need
about 2–3 minutes). Drain off the excess oil. Serve with vanilla ice cream
and the sauce.

rich chocolate *fudge*

INGREDIENTS

generous ¹/₄ cup raisins
2 tbsp rum
²/₃ cup milk
1 lb/450 g superfine sugar
3 tbsp unsalted butter, diced,
plus extra for greasing
3¹/₂ oz/100 g semisweet chocolate,
broken into small pieces
generous ³/₈ cup shelled pistachios,
chopped

SERVES 4

Grease an 8-inch/20-cm square baking pan.

Put the raisins in a bowl, pour over the rum, and set aside.

Heat the milk and sugar in a pan over low heat, stirring, until the sugar has dissolved. Add the butter and chocolate and stir until melted. Add the pistachios and the rum-soaked raisins and mix well. Bring gently to a boil, then cook over medium heat, stirring constantly, for 15–20 minutes.

Remove the fudge from the heat, press evenly into the prepared pan, and level the surface. Let cool completely, then cover with plastic wrap and let chill for at least 1 hour, or until firm. Remove from the refrigerator, turn out onto a cutting board, and cut into squares. Return to the refrigerator until required.

To serve, remove from the refrigerator and arrange on a serving plate, in paper cases if desired.

INGREDIENTS

4$^{1}/_{4}$ oz/120 g white chocolate,
  broken into small, even-size pieces
4 tbsp butter, softened to
  room temperature
2 tbsp heavy cream
$^{1}/_{2}$ tsp brandy
grated white chocolate, to decorate

white chocolate *truffles*

MAKES 20

Put the chocolate pieces into a heatproof glass bowl and place over a pan
of hot but not simmering water. When it starts to melt, stir gently until
completely melted. Do not overheat, or the chocolate will separate. Remove
from the heat and gently stir in the butter, then the cream and brandy. Let
cool, then cover with plastic wrap and let chill for 2–2$^{1}/_{2}$ hours, or until set.

Remove the chocolate mixture from the refrigerator. Using a teaspoon,
scoop out small pieces of the mixture, then use your hands to roll them into
balls. To decorate, roll the balls in grated white chocolate. To store, transfer
to an airtight container and let chill for up to 12 days.

INGREDIENTS

12¹/₂ oz/365 g semisweet chocolate

6 tbsp unsalted butter, plus extra
for greasing

1 tsp strong coffee

2 eggs

scant ³/₄ cup packed brown sugar

1¹/₂ cups all-purpose flour

¹/₄ tsp baking powder

pinch of salt

2 tsp almond extract

³/₄ cup shelled Brazils, chopped

⁷/₈ cup shelled hazelnuts, chopped

1¹/₂ oz/40 g white chocolate

chocolate temptations

MAKES 24

Preheat the oven to 350°F/180°C. Grease a large baking sheet. Put 8 oz/
225 g of the semisweet chocolate with the butter and coffee into a heatproof
bowl set over a pan of barely simmering water and heat until the chocolate
is almost melted.

Meanwhile, beat the eggs in a bowl until fluffy. Whisk in the sugar
gradually until thick. Remove the chocolate mixture from the heat and stir
until smooth. Stir into the egg mixture until combined.

Sift the flour, baking powder, and salt into a separate bowl and stir into the
chocolate mixture. Chop 3 oz/85 g of the remaining semisweet chocolate
into pieces and stir into the mixture. Stir in the almond extract and nuts.

Put 24 rounded dessertspoonfuls of the mixture onto the prepared baking
sheet and bake for 16 minutes. Transfer to a wire rack to cool.

To decorate, melt the remaining semisweet chocolate and white chocolate
in turn, spoon into a pastry bag, and pipe lines onto the cookies.

white chocolate *cake*

CAKE
butter, for greasing
4 eggs
$^2/_3$ cup superfine sugar
generous $^3/_4$ cup all-purpose flour, sifted
pinch of salt
$1^1/_4$ cups heavy cream
$5^1/_2$ oz/150 g white chocolate, chopped

CHOCOLATE LEAVES
$2^3/_4$ oz/75 g semisweet or white chocolate,
melted (see page 91)
handful of rose leaves, or other small edible
leaves with well-defined veins,
washed and dried

SERVES 4–6

To make the chocolate leaves, brush the melted chocolate over the undersides of the leaves. Arrange, coated-sides up, on a baking sheet lined with parchment paper. Let chill until set, then peel away the leaves.

Preheat the oven to 350°F/180°C. Grease and line an 8-inch/20-cm round cake pan. Put the eggs and sugar into a heatproof bowl and set over a pan of simmering water. Whisk until thick, remove from the heat and whisk until cool. Fold in the flour and salt. Pour into the prepared pan and bake for 20 minutes, then let cool for 10 minutes. Turn out, discard the lining paper, and let cool.

Put the cream into a pan over low heat and bring to a boil, stirring. Add the chocolate and stir until melted. Pour into a bowl, cover with plastic wrap, and let chill overnight.

Cut the cake horizontally in half. Whisk the chocolate cream until thick, spread one-third over one half of the cake, and top with the other half. Coat with the remaining chocolate cream. Let chill for 1–2 hours, decorate with chocolate leaves, and serve.

index